REACHING THE SHORE
OF THE SEA OF FERTILITY

REACHING THE SHORE
OF THE SEA OF FERTILITY

POEMS

ANNA LAURA REEVE

Fort Smith, Arkansas

REACHING THE SHORE OF THE SEA OF FERTILITY

Cover image © Samantha Farmer
Author photograph © Jessica Tezak

Edited by Casie Dodd
Design & typography by Belle Point Press

Belle Point Press
Fort Smith, Arkansas
bellepointpress.com
editor@bellepointpress.com

Printed in the United States of America

27 26 25 24 23   1 2 3 4 5

Library of Congress Control Number: 2023930201

ISBN: 979-8-9858965-8-9

RSSF/BPP10

Contents

Ars Poetica

Getting up early to stare
into my Himalayan salt lamp, to float on the silence
of 6:15 a.m., is one kind of meditation.
It is my only space to think.

I write four lines, and my husband's alarm
goes off. It must be time
to wake my daughter, make the lunches
I didn't make last night.

Domestic poem. No hunts,
no kills. But here on a steel rail,
frozen, till painful to the touch,
and miles from civilization, I put my ear.

I

The Edinburgh Postnatal Depression Scale

The most common measure to screen for depression related to childbearing is the EPDS. This self-report instrument contains ten items ranked from 0 to 3 that reflect the patient's experience over the past week. The EPDS has been validated extensively for use in the postpartum period.
—Dorothy K. Sit, MD, and Katherine L. Wisner, MD, MS

1. *I have been able to laugh
   and see the funny side of things*

   Steel, so much steel, and cold
   since the heat in the delivery room was either off or sweltering.
         The husband faded behind pain, reappeared,   again faded.

   Then I was close enough to see over the cliff of terror and jumped—

   she was out of my skin and in the world. She opened one gray eye.
      Who   in the world

            One more thing, OB talking again, *blood clotted*
        in uterus,   bring it out by hand,
   this will hurt,

   and fingers—blocky man's fingers—swept me,
        like when you empty your bag into the trash,
            scooping, shaking, I was,
       body flexed tight as a bowstring, teeth crushed together
   for how long how long, then chattering
         and very cold.

   She cried like she was hoarse—just whispers.

   They pricked her heel every two hours, squeezing out her blood.

Lying beside us, my husband looked over at her
and she was blue—   only for a moment.

Have I laughed? I smiled a lot at people who smiled at me.

If something funny were to happen, I would laugh, I think. Nothing funny
has happened.

2. *I have looked forward to things*
   with enjoyment

   —as much as I ever did,
   though I deliberate over this statement
   with confusion, and a familiar
   sense of dread.

   In the center of my body is a river
   of fear and whispering;

   unknown shapes and sharp edges
   slowly roil.

   At the hospital
   I broke open, exposing the wincing skin
   of a baby, three weeks early, to cold air
   and bright lights. I was sorry for her,
   so sorry.

   The midwives had bragged
   about their discharge time: 4 hours
   after delivery. *You'll want to be home.*

   After the baby turned blue,
   then pink again, and my milk hadn't come in,
   I knew differently. My husband more rattled
   than I. His Ménière's diagnosis, strange symptoms
   of tinnitus, balance problems, deafness
   casting a slowly-ballooning shadow.

When he goes back to work in a week,
I thought, I'll be completely alone
with this

my own body sewn back together with steel
or plastic, still bleeding.

3.   *I have blamed myself unnecessarily*
     when things went wrong

     I have blamed myself correctly
     when things went wrong.

     I'm a marionette,
     limping home with a blown glass infant
     balanced on my wooden arms.

4. *I have been anxious or worried*
   for no good reason

A new picture window suddenly cut
        in the corner of the house. Private rims
  and edges cast plainly in naked light,
the mind tired and redrawing, feebly, in new
          flashes of illumination.

Our new rental turned out to be a half-buried rusty bucket:
     galvanized steel top above a lace
  of uneven brown teeth, deep in soil.

     Attic flies emerged in a warm February
but camel crickets and cockroaches scoured the floors
  every night. Earwigs scuttled
        by the living-room baseboards.
     Twice I found slugs on the kitchen toe-kicks.

Yes I've been anxious and worried
for very good reasons—babies stop breathing
      without warning
  I am shredded and unstable
in my pelvis and there are roaches there are slow
    black flies like carrion flies.

I saw a sign inside the birth center's bathroom door:
     Sleep deprivation has been linked to PPD!
       Make sure you're sleeping!

But at the hospital they told me to feed her every 2 hours
till she reached her birth weight,

                                they said *breast is best*
                    so I latched her every 2 hours night
and day.

                    It took 2 weeks. I slept, woke
            to her raw cry,
                        nursing pillow buckled around me
            like a soft closed cervix.

5. *I have felt scared or panicky for no*
   very good reason

A rat ran up the clock and set me at 10:30,
ready to strike the half-hour, looking dead
at midnight. But the minute-hand tripped,
knocking forward then back, unable to crest
the gear's tooth. I would begin to relax
when a whimper crackled from the baby monitor,
its red light flaming. In my body, a rubber band
stretched to a paler shade of chalky white.
Our house was a safe house: a bunker with earth
piled up to high windows. That explained the slugs
and earwigs, the gunshots cracking at dusk.
I imagined a man with a gun breaking in, both of us
sitting up in bed, our faces masks of tragedy,
and there he was, between us and the baby.
I sat nursing her and rocking, her cheeks softer
than any known substance, gold lashes fluttering
open and closed, with the clear sense that I
was the officer chosen through some cataclysmic
chain of events to guard this baby, parents dead,
placed in the care of a witness protection program.
I remember the day this metaphor came to me.
Epiphany: the right word entering the cloud, releasing
meaning in a downpour of clarity. One knot came
undone, then three, then a draft of clean air riffled
the pages of my Encyclopedia of Threats,
ponderous as a family Bible and lying open
on its spine.

6. *Things have been getting on top of me*

But the baby cries so much of the time.
I can't think of exactly when or how long,
I just feel so sorry for her little body
that hurts somewhere. When I step into
the familiar lift and go all the way down
to a basement room with a high small
window and nurse her to sleep, her blue eyes
look up at me with interest and a peace
I want. I want a body to lie on, to be held.
I worry there's sadness in my milk. There's not.
But it makes me weep. She watches me,
latched and curious, hand light as a leaf
brushing my collarbones and breasts.
Sometimes she's restless and I grit my teeth
and rock so hard the springs groan. Her whines
quiet as she feels the relief of inertia. So do I.
As she sleeps, I open the screenlock
of my phone so I can see other people
through its little window. I'll only be free
for an hour, and I am only a little free.

7. *I have been so unhappy*
   that I have had difficulty sleeping

For weeks, now, I've been so tired
that I have difficulty thinking.

I've been so chilled by the baby's cry
that I have difficulty keeping

it together. Late on her worst nights,
instead of humming lullabies

I have raged-paced, clutching her
in my arms, and I have been so unhappy.

When she sleeps, I've been so relieved
that my sleep comes easily. Dreamless

and heavy, a perfect oblivion,
at night but never day.

I'm having trouble with conditional
statements. But if rage is idiopathic,

it should be secret. I think. I'm uncertain.
I'll offer another statement in its place:

I have been so somnambulant
that often, I put the baby in her carseat

then drive 40 miles down
the interstate, and 40 miles back.

8. *I have felt sad or miserable*

She's been out of my body for a week.

I'm glad

she's still alive. I'm not glad

that a blanket

thrown over our naked bodies

is too much heat for her.

What I need is to sleep with her on my chest (I long for it),

but I wake to find her body hot,

not sweating, 102F.

I call my mother, shaking. I wipe the baby with wet cloths,
making her cry.

Why should my heart's blood be too hot for her
when she was robed in it

seven days ago?

But things will get easier—which things I don't know—

and then we will both be happy.

9. *I have been so unhappy*
   that I have been crying

Only occasionally does pain or crying
                happen to me. Most of the time

                        I feel the chill and open space
        of awe but without the joy.

Quite often
        my canoe slides down a river

                        of threat, a low sky
                boxing us in,
                                        strange forms
                        moving under us.

Often, a goblin crouching behind me sings
grim fairy tales in one ear. I scan the floor for roaches
        with one eye.

        Husband's vertigo laps the gunwhales,
                        tinnitus screaming like a jet engine
                                only he can hear.

        In the night, her cry boxes our ears
like the gunshot

                we heard last night from
                        the next street over.
                                        We string
                        our nerves around the perimeter
                of the bedroom
        to cast a soft glow.

10. *The thought of harming myself has*
     occurred to me

When you first gave me this test,
the day after my body ran aground on a reef
and pushed out a baby, not a single thought
had occurred to me. Only this shipwreck,
its two bloodied survivors.

When you gave me this test again,
first pediatrician's visit at 2 weeks,
I knew what you wanted me to say.
Everyone firm and efficient, and I, a ghost
not entirely embodied, was expected to raise
a human child and, if possible, to get
inside the walls of the cheerful city.

First, the thought never, ever occurred to me.

Second, when I drove her to sleep
every afternoon—freedom of the mind if not
the body—blank mugshots of unhappy mothers
occurred to me, and I recognized them.
My arms so tired I held the wheel with one hand
at a time.

Months later, I allowed it to occur to me
that relief, rightness, and completeness
was a ramp into the sky as the sun set above the interstate,
all three of us exiting our terrible life
in the same car at the same time: instantaneous.
What a drug.

To imagine the end with neither pain nor survivors.

Sometimes, during endless nursing sessions,
      I imagined the solidity and peace
   of lying in a roomy box
         under spring topsoil.

   Nothing to pull
or push me, fight me, ask anything of me, or cry
      these terrible sad cries.   I've been fighting
with the husband over housework in the daytime
        and we've been screaming. In the night,

the baby cries. Under
   the earth

I could lie perfectly still, be perfectly silent. I think
I hear rain falling.

        Above me, earthworms
   and tiny centipedes tunnel. Grubs rest
     in their little caves.

   I feel around me the light curtains
of roots, working in their diligent way, unaware
of me.

Driving the Baby

Breaks in winter clouds
   like grease films in dishwater.

     Carseat back-facing
baby in its gentle mouth, lion-tamer,
       her tiny head
     demonstrating how domestic

Little hatchback, your large headlights
   like mouse eyes;

little coffee here, little there,
     my life tiny, my life tiny
       underneath
        these dry strata.

Open to my hands,
   open to my eyes
  fault of living.

Huddled copper coins
       in a secret dish;

  scarlet and salmon fabric roses tufting
    the snow-covered graves
   as we glide by in our elevator
 of glass.

First Unbroken Sleep

After four and a half hours of unbroken sleep
    I feel like a swan

The 'trying to conceive' web forum
recedes into the past, where every missed period
was a cause for dreams
    and good lucks were *baby dust!* with
                rotating star gifs.

Good luck wishes in the new mom groups
    are *sleepy dust.*
    These women who parted Red Seas to look
into small slate-gray eyes—
on their seventh day they want to sleep.

While for me, filament-thin sprays of milk arc
    and lie on my daughter's eyelids
        as I cajole her awake.

    Seven weeks in the amusement park,
seven weeks sleeping in the operator's booth
waking to my baby whining
in her sleep,
        my shirt a wet hood
over two fawns' faces.

Ménière's Disease

My tea is steeping.
Windchimes clatter whitely on the porch,

banks of bamboo bow
and shoulder into the wind

The inner ear, its coils
its mazes

I forget for a moment which way
the letter z faces, and write it backwards.

The tiny hairs of the innermost ear,
so innermost it is almost
the brain, so innermost we almost don't believe in it,

send messages in Morse code:
dizzy dizzy vertigo
nystagmus dizzy ess oh ess oh ess

Husband crouched over the toilet for hours,
then, recovered, driving to work
on gray highways, for hours.

Degenerative and *idiopathic* means
he is losing his hearing.
That orienting light for the eyes
in the back of the head,

repository
for the alphabet of degrees between music
and silence.

Sleeping Apart

When our daughter was new we slept apart,   he on the couch and I on the bed,
bouncing her to sleep on a spring   I woke with every chirp, squeak, or cry
His inner ear disease was progressing—   we thought he would soon be deaf
in both ears, unable to drive   or reliably work   —he hunched in the bathroom
for 3 hours of vertigo,   vomiting   holding his head perfectly still
with his hands over the toilet   retching after moaning   moaning
after retching   small times of quiet groaning   when maybe
it was   ebbing,   but then   it ratcheted up again   and I was pacing
the house with the two-month-old in my arms   All I knew was   not to
drop her   so I didn't—every inch of her firmly held   I went to the bedroom
        to feed her and I did not even believe that milk was coming out of me
I wished,   dry-mouthed,   for her not to starve   at my breast   This
is the memory I didn't want   I took a photo the next morning
of his happy face beaming over our doll-sized baby,   his eyes swollen
with sleep,   cheeks   flushed with happiness.

Yoga Nidra after Trauma

The silence of heaven
bears down infinitely

heavier than the noise
of earth. Beads of light

scatter, leaving the crush,
equilibrium between ex- and im-

plosion. It rests between the thin
ridges of my shoulder blades.

Corpse. Time sunders,
a susurrus like citrus carpels

separating. How is it that silence
is alive, and so bright?

They told me to crack open,
to splay, to dilate

the pupil and to cup
the ear, as if what came from heaven

was a play of shadows
or a faint strain of music.

Exile

Paper pure as the snow at our park,
        pock-marked only
    by feet of joy

After convalescence
    these long strings of happiness

She sleeps in the carseat, unbelievably still
        while outside the car, slate gravel, blue shadow
tawny broomsedge   and olive-green river

How do I find my way,
winter of seclusion, nosebleeds,
                and this baby who
        is always with me

Even watching birds is denied me,
                even walking by the river

Black dog, catch the tennis ball
    your simple body
            running away and back

Woman in a red down-filled coat,
        throw the ball
            with a launcher, wander
            in the snow

Everything be just as it is
Everyone remain just as you are

Postal worker, come to the river
            with your lunch
        and gaze into the light

II

Trying

Leaving the party on a pretext,
I return to the second-story apartment.

I could walk out of each window
onto hackberry branches,

or emerge from the bedroom skylight, dimmed
with rainwater deposits and fine cracking,
into the crown of a hackberry.

What do people want, when they want
children? Souls

from the next world, or the previous.

Maybe our lives have not yet been lived.
Maybe our lives have never
been lived.

Little shoots, little eggs,
you wither

and go down with the massa damnata
to the place where the unformed
rest.

In my pelvic cavity
the wheel of the seeder spins,
dropping eggs in furrows. At the farm
I seed clover, vetch,
rye, and oats over four acres

but nothing comes up in the fall,
or our warm southern winter.

A flock of doves bursts into flight
as we drive past—did they eat the seed?
Did early warmth coax the shoots out
and then kill them with hard frosts?

It's the end of March and the martins
and red-winged blackbirds are back.
A song sparrow tunes
a bow-like syrinx.

My basil seedlings keel over
one after the other, damping off.

Our farmer says, "Healthy plants can fight pests."
"Healthy soil doesn't need fertilizer
in the growing season," she says.

When the farm's bright February seedlings
faded pink and purple in the greenhouse, starved
by nutrient-poor potting media, we started over,

adding handfuls of fertilizer,
soaking new shoots in fish emulsion.
Direct-seeded, though it was early.

Tiny seed leaves, opening yourselves, undaunted,
to the glow of my apartment grow-lamp,
what do you want to be?

Another Thing They Don't Tell You

Serving bedhead chic in black-and-white
leggings and Keds boots, I walk
from the parking garage to the hospital
for bloodwork after the Misoprostol
and *schloomp* from dilated cervix
a jellied clot the size of a child's hand
slithers hot from me and is caught
THANK GOD, I AM THANKING YOU
WHEREVER YOU ARE
in my expandable foam XL pad
that crinkled when I walked, like a diaper,
and now is silent and perspiring
under its heavy load. Oh little horse—
how faithful—we shuffle into
a nurse's bathroom to unsaddle.
I'm shaken. All I can think to do is take
a photo in case my doctor asks questions
I can't answer. I don't know
what I'm looking at. I wrap and drop it
into the trash. It falls heavily,
like a wallet.

Sprouting Wand

you are like the branches of the dying peach tree
we piled in early spring by the fire ring,
bare, buds. Two weeks later,
tiny green tongues and pink flowers
festooned them.

I wanted them to stop—horrible,
in some way, for dead branches to bloom.
There they lay, not conserving
their little sap, their little dignity,
making a flowered circlet
for a grave, determined and knowing.

They moved according to the motion
of the natural world: spend what you have
on flowers, and it will return to you
seeds.
        In another week,
they faded, but bees had still come
to them.

Playing the Washboard

Birdsong thins the air.
       Liquid calls from cardinals criss-cross
           the yard like plumes of woodsmoke
   or steam from a hot cup, lit by sunrise.

I am so still
    that a brown thrasher and her fledgling
  alight in the garden near me
      to pick through the leafmulch.

    Dark chest streaks I see so rarely—
     sign of a forest dweller—
another staccato, another dash of pepper.

Splattering of hackberry buds thickly
      gathering overhead,
    wet streaks of boxelder tassels smearing.

I wait for the rain to begin
  and send me back inside.
Here in our city, and in yours, the pandemic.

  Here the female bluebird,
neutral-colored, with just enough blue;
     here the buzzy call of the Carolina wren
like somebody playing the washboard.

Thinking Big

Warm spring mornings awaken the carpenter bees
      wintering in the shed plywood,
   twenty-five or thirty of them
         tangling mid-air, hypervigilant,
       chasing, grappling,
staccato bounced on a fiddle string.

     I sit and watch them, great
         eighty-year old pines and maples
    lifting in the distance.
     I wonder if I can survive
   each small horror.

The husband, up late, comes to sit beside me,
   balancing eggs and toast on his lap
and coffee on the arm of his folding chair.
       The coffee spills, entirely,
      he barks *GODDAMMIT* and throws
     his plate into the yard,
   walks back inside without looking back.

I'm pregnant. Above me
     a knot of carpenter bees, interrupted
   by the through-flight of a cardinal,
         forget their squabble, and chase it.

In the Garden, Watching the Storm Come In

A green lynx spider rests
atop echinacea bristles,
spined legs drawn up into a crouch.

Distant thunder unrolls its rug,
and to the east, dark rays of rain
shine from slate clouds.

I hope the winds aren't bad.
My three rows of Cherokee corn
are chest-high and still unhilled.

A vee of Canada geese
heads toward the storm,
talking urgently amongst itself,

and cumulostratus begins to thin above me,
revealing the thunderhead, summit
impossibly high, lit blush

and apricot in the dawn,
appearing like Mount Mitchell on
a beneficent day.

Notes on the Balds of Southern Appalachia

Shrubs encircle this mountaintop   like a monk's tonsure.
I imagine this bald in 1820—   a herd of short-horned cows
driven up 4,600 feet by dogs and   farmhands on horseback.
At the summit, they folded knobbed   legs and didn't stand
for an hour, shaking crickets from   wet flanks,
staring at the shadows beneath   Mount Mitchell
and stars emerging, twenty   at a time.

My friend says that horses   tear up the ground,
won't move from a patch of   grass till they have torn out
the roots. Cows, he says,   take better care of sod.
Maybe this is why the balds   of our mountains light
on us with a sparrow's weight: occasionally,
we can appreciate a careful   animal.

Forest is reclaiming the   grassy balds of the mountains
to the west, a park managed   by federal order. Spring pumps
and smokehouses at Greenbriar   and Cades Cove dissolve
beneath leaf litter. Blueberry barrens   harbor beech saplings
on Andrew's Bald, covering the hogpen   footprint, the
hunting cabin, overwriting pasture   and cropland,
starting the forest clock over   at zero.

On Max Patch, in a Pisgah forest   held
by more lenient strictures, wild   snapdragons
survive each summer mowing   and multiply.
It's September. Goldenrod   and ironweed
freckle the hilltop. Cricketsong   shimmers
at our knees, laps against the   rainfly all night.
The murmur of voices   loosens like smoke.

First Sugar Moon of the Pandemic

Chickweed and bird's eye speedwell recede,
                 the tiny white teeth and blue water
      of their flowers
giving way to hairy bittercress, purple dead-nettle. White tufts
         flanked by dark javelins rise
      beside dragon heads.

Maple sap drips from sapsucker holes, and the green troll-hair
         of onion grass pocks the lawn

    while each answering cardinal call
        splatters the air with a thin
      iridescent paint, here and gone.

When they decide it's spring, it's spring. Calendar be damned.

Now, year-old sage will sprout leaves
    from root crowns. Honeysuckle bushes
        will crack their green fireworks.

Yonder,
a robin has been trying for ten minutes
    to break a beakful of shredded polypropylene twine
    from its tangle
  on a tomato cage.

Agricultural twine now appears in the nests
    of an increasing number of birds, who love it
  for its flexibility and strength,
        who often fly in search of it, whose feet
  it entangles,
    whose hatchlings

it orphans. Even chicks
  get tangled, limbs becoming deformed.

This is not a poem about survival.

  The robin stops tugging
and perches on the cage wire,
        preening.

In a moment, I will go to the tangle
    and she will fly away, while I cut the white
  threads from the wire, crushing them
in my hand.

Dawn with Holy Basil

Charmingly aggressive holy basil,
you fill out your allotted space and more.

You tinge damp unmoving air with the color
of your scent.

Over there
are the things I should have done.
Deprived of my lifeblood, they shrivel.

Over there is the empty horizon
blushing peach, the work
of trees blackly written. Around me
stands a mist, I'm damp with it, and now,
the first robin call.

A catbird calls
a hoarse morning mew.

It will be 95 degrees today and tomorrow,
and on Halloween. When they should
be robed in wookie furs
or encased in cardboard,
kids will get hot and shed costume pieces
like Icarus.

Meanwhile the holy basil shoulders aside
rosemary, valerian, and lavender
so its large wings can open.

Red-Tailed Hawk

Ten minutes' stillness in the shade garden
and the smoke of birdsong rises around me.

Chipping, twittering, hoarse croaks.
Dee dee dee and *hey, sweetie* from the thicket.

Jays, chickadees, crows. The sharp *pit*
of sap dropping on leaf litter. A song sparrow's

ambitious motif, the eerie whistle of a starling.
Broomsedge clumps stand thin and isolated

in the winter lawn—tawny, arcing gracefully,
fingers full of tufted seed. Like Ceres,

body a stook of golden sheaves. These grains
feed only songbirds—finches, cardinals.

Far above, a red-tailed hawk is weaving,
pursued by four screaming crows, who dive

one at a time to pluck at flight feathers
and tail. It sends a piercing shriek tumbling

across the valley, unmistakable in timbre,
harsh and reedy, a sound we have come

to associate with desolation. Our own,
or—more often—of others. But she rolls

like a seal, tail fanned and glowing like embers.

Vegetable X

Garlic leaves   stand in a grid   satisfying   as lattice-top pie
Nothing in my life stays   where I put it   like these
          A hard tug leaves green juice on the hand   broad
    spreading roots cling to soil   like a hank of hair to scalp
Unbrowsed by deer   groundhog   rabbit   yes,
hallelujah   I say it before Easter,   I say it
when I want   I say it   to the volatile sulphur
compounds   that address   the olfactory   elicit
a moan   then with a sly smile, split clove open   and glistening
say   *wanna do it again?*   Garlic   delicious slut
  I grow you   to lick   your lovely   clit   I come
out to watch you   grow your sprouts   in December
  your thick shaft   in March   your sixth leaf
in April   your juice running in May,   and in June I pull one
  plant   to see your pink wrappers drying   tattered   I peel
a pale bulb   with my thumb   each small mound
  tumescent   alive   arcing   with pleasure

Tennessee Red Cob

Grasping the bound ear with the heel of my left hand,
I pierce the top shucks with both thumbs, punching open a slit.
Dry husks rip with a groan and squeak as the great creamy teeth
gleam. Another hard tug frees the whole magnificent horn of plenty.

Dented kernels neatly aligned or occasionally shoepegged—a word
that looks like the jumble it means—sit jammed tight and topfull
as a flush of button mushrooms. I love this corn for its gravitas:
heavy as milk glass, alive as an animal. Its meal, light as wheat flour.

Maíz, elote, late daughter of corn mother, let me never guess
your secret. You know mine: hunger, and awe. Within them, you
continue your ancestors' work of 9,000 years at your own behest.

And let me pull another ear open again—pink husks billowing
like skirts—rubbing ivory kernels free until your red furry cob
rests in my hands, glittering faintly, light as a twig.

For Southern Appalachia

i. On the skin, the bruise keeps no secrets. It tells
    of the impact, the rupture. In a body—in a year—
    when illness and fears of illness huddled, preparing
    to break out, I wished for a manifestation—or wells
    of silence. I went outside, where all I could hear
    were the urgent concerns of budding, breeding things
    on whose scaffolding we hang, beating our chests.
    It shudders or buckles, evolves not quite in our favor,
    and look at us—stockpiling, tacking without bearings—
    while mourning doves and brown thrashers build nests
    in riverbank grape and honeysuckle thickets.
    A single seed on fractured bedrock sings.
    A carpenter bee who will die this year rests
    on rosemary blooms in another eternal spring.

ii. On rosemary blooms in another eternal spring
    bilabiate corollas open their fleshy jaws:
    tiny crowd of dragon lantern dancers, lipped
    above and below, purple stigma arcing
    like frozen spurts of fire, or icy claws.
    Lavender sends up a phalanx of stems tipped
    with spearlike buds. Again, my placenta creates
    a witches' brew of hormones—nausea gnaws
    and gnaws—while an embryo, still and undeveloped,
    will develop no more. But the signal is lost. It waits.
    Life unrolls at our feet in the spring, and nothing
    escapes the wild zeal of its pollen, nor me, except
    the nectar-robbing bee, who cuts the bait
    from a long-necked flower, ovum bypassed, stripped.

iii. From a long-necked flower, ovum bypassed, stripped
of its little lick of nectar, a new lick wells.
Now long-tongued bumblebees and honeybees
will rob the bloom, too, through this hole punched
low on the throat, by the nectaries. The body culls
the malformed part, says *Hold still, honey, please*
and *Trust the process, baby girl* and *Fuck,*
I got nothing. This after six white Misoprostols.
Two years after the miscarriage, carpenter bees
emerge again. A two-year cycle of luck
and recovery done, this shameless nectar-robbing
is now part of me. Fertility, you're a tease.
Beggar. Thief. Magician. *I'm done, Puck.*
Go make daffodils and celandine poppies.

iv. *Go make daffodils and celandine poppies*
grow in the woods, by flame azalea and paw-paw.
Raze invasive wintercreeper and privet,
no longer newcomers—now endemic—freeze
the march of Japanese honeysuckle thicket, draw
down its early-leafing shade and give it
poison, dissolve its roots and burn its pith.
Bury the berries where none will grow or thaw.
I crack with incantations. Lightning. Then pivot-
ing, cedar smudge smoking aloft, the monolith
divides again. There is no Tanasi anymore.
The Overhill is overrun; each wormhole and divot
is planted, each thicket is vining and twisted with
colonizing species, like daffodils, here so long we forgot.

v.   Colonizing species, like daffodils, here so long we forgot.
       And how is it possible to overstate our newcomer
       status? Canopies of ancient forests haven't,
       nor mycorrhizal colonies, nor the catbird's obdurate
       fury as she chased me down the alley last summer,
       flitting nearer, strident *meah! meah!* and the glint
       of her black eyes so vengeful I laughed, then ran.
       Her species has nested here always. Latecomer,
       I represent siege, her ultimate displacement.
       I brought daffodils, yarrow. Blood and broadleaf plantain
       fill my footprints. The work of millennia tilts—
       we stagger, shift our weight—and the extinction event
       of our century crowns at Gaea's lips, a new Titan,
       as I watch towhees in the cedars, eyes black as flint.

vi.   As I watch towhees in the cedars, eyes black as flint,
       I return to my body. The ribcage of Earth still rises
       and falls beneath me. Calls of mockingbird and wren
       weave a lattice of sweet, sharp splints around me. Lent
       performs its pilgrimage to antiquity, littering crises
       of diet and disordered eating across the nation,
       while above, a bluebird pair takes turns diving low
       for insects, rising, tracing an ouroboros. It suffices.
       Blood thickens on uterine walls for two weeks, then
       sheds. The ouroboros belongs to me, and the crow,
       cicada, and scoliid wasp. Life's birthright is
       to live forever, to arc high over death, then bend
       hard into it, and die forever. But oh
       may it live a little, little longer, till then.

vii. May it live a little, little longer, till then-
      stunted sassafras saplings, transplanted in the corner
      where wintercreeper and honeysuckle hells
      once mounded, root in and green this place again.
      This chapped cheek. This Windy Moon's first quarter.
      This beat of color after graynumb like blood vessels
      filling in a strangled limb suddenly freed—this juice
      and gasp. Intermediate wood ferns beneath the cedar
      glow yellow in a shaft of light, sprays of bright pinnules
      on black jeweler's velvet. Resolute, I reintroduce
      these species, though now I think of coal companies
      grading bedrock and clay after mountaintop removals,
      then seeding fescue. But I can bear to see the bruise
      on the skin. The bruise keeps no secrets: it tells.

The Children of Asylum Seekers

Simple removal of child from parents fleeing fire.
Simple wrapping of woman, mother,
man, father, in wire.

Inside white tents, crèches
of brown children mill,

waiting for the feeling of
recognition to flood their bodies.

All we know of our parents is in the body: I knew
my mother's breast, because it was there that I turned outward
to see the world. It was my floor.

I knew my father's chest because for a while
my weakness fit there, like a soft body
under hard wing casings.

Pivoting in Appalachia

Through shaded classroom windows can I see
red and sugar maple inflorescence
tasseling high above drifts of cherry
    and saucer magnolia scurf.

Burnished carmine whirligigs on strings,
 chartreuse pedicels growing yellow
        with pollen—

        millions of tiny parts confusing the eye at a distance;
            nearer, unspooling like fractals.

Two more days till the end of March
and the cracking of the chocolate egg
        that will drip with caramel, covering
                all our sins. It is Lent,

        but Southern Appalachia has always observed
            with ireless green grass
    and glistering fleshy petals, sepals cracked
                and spread eagle.

Not even once
have I heard my Montessori preschoolers told
    that they have sinful hearts and dirty
                bodies.

Not once has a teacher asked them to imagine
being on fire with no mothers to help them,

            nor that a bearded man in a picture
        is the only one who can save them from a place
    where they are alone with a bad man   with horns.

Sophie Looks into My Eyes

Each hand rests on a child's back
in the classroom, gently rolling
little bodies to sleep. Behind my face
are storms over an ocean,
a dinghy streaming and dark.
Little feet, glitter sandal, flushed
cheek, and behind the velvet
brown eye of the child, looking
into my eye, shutters thrown open,
is another ocean. I see small boats
and that is all I can see.
Maybe she sees my little boat.
How dark my sea. I crouch
above it in a puddled stern
like a hawk on a thermal, swells
licking silent ribs, silent sternum,
guitars and toca shell rattle
on the classroom speaker ebbing
and rising like tides.

Look at Everything

Springscent lifts on the last day of February.
The complex formations of Lent bunching
to the west, Putin's war to the east. Grape hyacinth
and purple deadnettle open miniscule lips
with a *puh* and each efflux is so sweet
bees will find it. On my run this morning,
the rain-swollen stream released vapor overhead
like a little blindness. Obscurity. Fragrance.
I thought, as I ran, of the Ukrainian teacher
photographed as she taught students sheltering
in a Kyiv subway. How much easier it is
to teach spelling rules or animal life cycles
than to explain murder to a child. Once,
I tried to tell my daughter of an assassination
but found myself plummeting, suddenly,
to the foot of the mountain. How does a mother,
father, teacher, or anyone who loves a child,
puncture the seal, allowing safety and death
to taste each other's breath. It is the difficult work
of the child to observe. It is the work of the teacher
to say *Look at everything, then look again at me.*

Yard-Sitting during the Pandemic

Yellow-jacket, tiny
poison packet, swings like a censer,
wafting awareness between every grass clump.

After a night of little sleep, thick cloud cover.
Breezes too slight to be registered by trees
make the grasses quiver.

Apples fall from the tree badly split by storm.
Heavy, dimpled by insects, mottled
and thinly striped, thump.

                    The belly of the yard rises
            and falls. I perch on it
               in a folding chair,

   teetering for a moment,
until I set my coffee down, finding the correct
center of gravity.

There are none so evil
that grass dies under their feet.

When the neighbor's cat wandered in, a mockingbird flew low
            over its head, making a loud *chip* call, calling *chip,*
      chip, until the cat turned and walked away.

IV

Sleep Deprivation

Motherhood is putting a sock in it.
Putting a sock on it.
Motherhood is The Great Sock Hunt.

Curtains, pulling them.
Invisible warpaths my feet beat every day
but such little wars.

Motherhood is a visor I can't take off.
    Kids' TV show voice actors squeaking
        and scrambling, the little
           ha-has, merciless upward inflections.

Motherhood is a duststorm.
I tie scarves over our mouths and noses,
I yell *close the door!*
I see motes in the air, regardless.
The inside of my mouth, nose,
       is dry with fine layers
          of careful work,
fast work.

I walk across the yard as my daughter calls me
    and I know I will stay inside, now, and start dinner.

My head is a balloon
that wants to find its new form
    in those cumulonimbus up there,

          oh this sky. How wide it is.
How like an enormous bowl of light and cloud.

But with a hole in the unseeable center—
   if I loosed myself like a blue balloon
      I would roll,
     find a center,
    fall out.

Cooking while Daughter Demands Bananas

Purple cauliflower florets fade
from mauve to blue-violet,
my daughter clamors in her yellow way—
staccato flashes of orange, red—
and sweet potato matchsticks steam
from muskmelon to gold. Red onion
blunts, bleeds.

Mary want banana! from the counter
where she is standing on a toddler chair
and within a few moments' strategy
of knives.

A tangle of ocean floor flora spits
and hisses in a skillet so heavy I can barely lift it.
It grounds my lightning so that
Can I have a more banana!
doesn't provoke me,
my sea remains calm and blue.

Purple kale ribbons
wilt and release their violet,
folklorico ruffles turning forest green
on spines of magenta.

I feel that the window is open and calling
to my heart like a kite, but no:
mistaken. All is close about me,
stained violent colors
calming to odors, textures, abundance.

Even my daughter's copper hair
is still and gold
and not, as usual,
a cap of flame.

Entrapment

Reading poetry as a teenager, phrases
like "my daughter," "my son," or "as I fold laundry"
extinguished interest like the smell of shit. The firm thud
    of a diaper tossed in the trash
        seemed to echo.

  "Domestic tranquility" suffocated, like oil
on seawater.

 Second oldest of seven, my only scar from childhood
is a two-inch stripe on my knee from changing
    baby siblings on the floor, legs a wide V
with baby between my knees.

One time out of hundreds
    the pin cut forward too fast
        through the tripled cotton gauze,
the shallow Z motion of the needle tip scoring a
    red line, blushing only a little, hardening quickly.
My friends' scars were trophies of sport, scouting,
freedom. But secretly, I loved my domestic
        scar, because it meant I was needed
at home.
        When I made a daughter and lay down
    in the fitful sleep of new motherhood,
all I had was my daughter
  and the slime trails and greasy stains
of domestic tranquility.

Something in my body said *this again*
   and I fell in.
  So I add this to my work,
leaning at this wall of windows in my forehead,

cutting the paint that seals them shut
with a razor.

The Mad Mother Responds to Your Text

There is a time to tell the well-wishers
to go to hell. Or rather, to come to hell,
where you are toiling, waking & sleeping,
lifting your head occasionally to read the text
from your mother or comment from
your friend which says—invariably—
This too shall pass. Some feverishly print
the text & light it with a match over the trash,
but others—perhaps, you—will turn
a row of gleaming teeth on your friend
& beckon with a crooked finger: *Come
down here, the water is fucked.*

Humorously, on Eavan Boland's Children

Eavan Boland wrote in her home study
while her children played elsewhere in the house,
so it must be possible, and therefore
I'm going to begin a zenlike
practice of writing while my kid
sings and drops things and
tells me to *come look at this.*

In six months, when I have learned how
to say, *Wait my dear, mama is busy*
and then, *What is it my darling child?*
with tranquil calm and beatific poise,
then my daughter who yells *MAMA I POOPED*
pulling up her tights before I come skidding in
with a *Don't get up! Don't get up!* will recycle her waste
and poop no more. Then, my daughter
who can't find her purple bunny because she
did not look for it will have graduated from a course
in looking, and her certificate program in
Keeping Clothes On will have awarded her honors
in Clothes in Winter, and Pants Specifically.

It comes to mind that she can lack imagination.
Either that or I attachment-parented her.
In any case, she adheres to me like a burr.
I believe the only program for that is Malicious Snarling
which, as an attachment parent, I find unconscionable,
and of course I occasionally dabble.

Eavan Boland's children seem
to have played cheerfully and quietly,
and she seems to have spent serene

if troubled hours at her desk, staring out the window.
Were there any loud crashes? Entreaties,
or hissed threats? I see only a river
moving through her pale eyes.

Families Show Up at the Playground
on a Cold Afternoon in January

I come to the playground with my daughter
    at 1:10 in the afternoon, hoping to see human joy,
        a color, or a cloud of living breath.

Winter wastes paving a way to the horizon.
Blue sky blue as a bell.

    She pulls at me like a puppy, a puppy who talks
        and takes off coat hat and gloves,
    but as often happens, the playground is deserted,
since whatever other preschoolers do
    from 11:30am till 2:30pm is still going on,
        and this planet is still uninhabited.

Broad hillsides of dormant grasses increase.
    Blue sky fades
        with the hour. Sheetlike films
    of impersonal vapor form overhead.

    Was there a thing I had in mind

          ?

    ... .
  .. . .
      . ... . .

Up on the western slope the former asylum stands;
    a few offices, many floors of tall windows.
    White eyes wide: I see it
        surveilling the park

from its highest
point.

The slant of cloudcast grows more wan.

Daughter runs, circles back,
gloves back on, coat back on but unzipped,
snack box snapped open and shut again
and again.

At 3:00, a string of camels appears
on the horizon, roped jugs clattering, faintly,
some snorts, harness jingle. They come closer,
adult voices murmuring, the sound of children calling
to each other growing distinct.

Tall spaces of silence begin to thin,
and a sense of emptiness feels its lid taken off,
with a nearly-visible curl of updraft
like the white vapor of my breath
as I tip back my head to laugh
rising—ha

I'm alive

. aliv e

The Mad Mother Discovers a Third Way

Good mothers take care of everyone
else. *Bitch, defy it.* The broad way leads
into the River Styx, while the narrower way
goes overland, through mudpots & steaming pools
where you must put out little fires
daily till the end of time. A third way is defiance.
Difficult terrain, as defiance remains—
after all this time—a male virtue, & a factory
defect in women or children. In a mother,
it screams like a tornado siren.
                                    Since you
were taught to listen for a command,
to close your mouth & watch, ears pricked
like a dog, you need a voice to tell you
where to go. So command yourself.
The viral Facebook post telling of the mother
whose husband took the kids, saying
Go get coffee, take a break, you deserve it,
& she was so grateful that instead
she fetched donuts, like a good dog—?
It doesn't frighten you: it haunts you, like
the ghost of a toad. It stares at you
like a thing that will never die. It licks
an eyeball. But you will die. You're sick.
You're edging closer. Defy it. The voice
issuing apologies—allow it to fade.
The voice inviting the spirit to ascend
into the sternum—
Yes.

The Mad Mother Joins the Resistance

Below you is the rug, brimful of crumbs, & hairy:
the longer you imagine a ghost vacuum rolling,
screams of the damned whining from its mandible,
the neat row of popcorn kernels & shrunken
nubs it will deposit as soon as it is turned off,
the more of you is going to their place. Written
blackly on your wrist is "pick up CSA bin,"
"meal planning," "get groceries," & you sentence
yourself with those letters. Defy. Go to the sink,
mold-rimed with dark hairs lounging poolside & run
the cold water. Wash your face. Dry that bitch.
Say to whatever appears in the mirror, *Your work
is the real work. The real work is defiance.*
The fruit fly population in the kitchen: let it increase.
Your work is the real work. The complaints
of the husband & whining of the child: release
them like balloons. To be courteous, you may take
the strings; to be defiant, open your hand, allowing
them to float on the wind, the words becoming
unintelligible. The seven projects you started
that run under your feet in concrete pipes—
domesticated river, unable to flood & cracking
with accelerating chaos—thundering teeth from
your jaw, beating down stone walls & you are
shitting bricks because you fear they'll swallow you
whole—or abandon you forever—unbaptize them.
Dunk them in unholy water, pull your desire to you
backward through an anagram of dogma, make
what you want. Join the resistance. The work
will calm in your hands as you come with a bucket

of cold water, from tap, hose, or kiddie pool. Wet,
it returns to the river, & you are pouring water
into a daylighted river, returning self to self
as you forgot you could do.

New Myth

Combed out long on a diet
of Cinderella, Belle, and Rumpelstiltskin,
another generation of mothers
are cutting their tower-long braids
to pull themselves out of holes, wells, and ditches.
Becoming bitches. Begrimed, fucked,
and pissed. Hail, dirty witches.

Come wash your hair, whose strength
you have stolen in cutting it. Its dark
heavy mass becoming inert, falling away dead,
leaving you, elastic and alive.

Vasilisa

1. My mother gave me a wooden doll.
I feed it and it is a secret to me. I tap it:
nothing answers but the hollow *tok*
of a cedar dowel. When I leave my house,
the last candle snuffed, I hold in my hand
in the pocket of my jacket a thing that eats,
drinks, warns and blesses me. It flutters
like a curtain between me and a vast sea
of knowledge.

Once it had a fever and I wiped it with cool
water. I carry it, stumping along woodenly
in search of the light in the forest.

I set myself strange and endless tasks.
I sort poppyseeds from black soil and pick
molded kernels from buckets of corn,
like my mother the miller's daughter
who spun caverns of straw into gold. Like her,
I find the task impossible and somehow
done. Like her, I fear death.

But I fear neither crones nor witches.
Nor the ancient spirit who flies in a mortar,
magnificent ugliness standing above me
like a mountain—magnetic, unknown.

She knows my secret. She calls me lucky. Me,
a stranger to the day I was born and the day
I will die.

2. When I was good enough,
    irreproachable,
I asked for light to live by.
                    I did everything.
I was the white cow creamer
    on the antique bureau, I was the weed
            between stones.
What
was missing?   My house dark
    no matter the time, or day,   too dark
to see the gray glow beneath a curtain
or hand
    before my face.
            I heard this proverb:

When you don't know where you're going,
go by a way you don't know.

I ate it. It clung to me like a burr in fine hair.
    I sent myself out.

The old witch, older than sin
    or good, older than anything
    I have seen   or felt
gave me a torch of ulna and skull,
            light flaming
                from orbits and nasal fossae.

            It was my terror
        and my light.

I waited for it to burn me to ashes.
In the bedroom glass, I saw the image
    of a woman, visage cut—bladed—intent
as a wolf, hungry and ready to feed
herself.

V

The Work of Mothers

A mother has a soul.
A soul needs

to walk uninterrupted down the train
and through each car,

emerging alone at the balcony
of the last car, steel shrieking,

black night opening
suddenly like a blade

or black parachute, sucking loose hats, change,
dust, into it,

divulging nothing. A soul
has seasons.

It practices death and rebirth. Its hair
grows lush,

then sheds; its love fills, then empties;
it dies absolutely

to the ground, but a root persists; or,
even roots wither

in drought, but a seed-case
swells—

then shatters—
dropping one seed.

A door slides open. White bones
turn, lightened & expressionless,

to re-enter the last car.

The Mad Mother Envies a Window

Solitude is necessary for the artist. For the child,
it is necessary to return to the womb.

The artist who is a mother splits herself in two.

The womb makes space. It raises the child
over and over again, like the man who trained
his chihuahua to trot the midline of his body
as he turned somersault after somersault.
According to the manual, this can continue
forever. Meanwhile, beauty lifts in the distance
like cumulonimbus—heavy, never raining.
The window frames it. The window
is the artist.

The soul tries to do it with one leg, one eye,
in ten-minute increments every six business days
because the child is climbing, talking, and
trying to return to the womb. *Defy it.* She
cannot fit in the womb—she was too large
the instant she emerged, and that is why
she emerged.
                A task—
as momentous as comforting the child
who can no longer float in bespoke baths—
is taking the needles of your craft and stitching
yourself together.

Children Are Not the Glue

A towhee says 'sree' somewhere
and I agree. Spring tips toward summer,
balanced on one knuckle and full
of pleasure.

Ten foamflower stems arc high above flat leaves,
open like kids' hands, asking for something.

Putting thoughts of my 4-year-old aside,
I draw the breath that kindles
beneath my sternum, and re-enter the world.

How content, in this place, is each thing
to be what it is. Carolina wrens waiting for a calm
to sing their voluble songs.

Towering maples and hackberries solid
and strange as sliding boulders in the Sahara—
both speaking and secret.

Jays and mockingbirds not caring who knows it.

My heart goes one way, my body goes another.
Children are not the glue to keep them together.

The towhee pair keep a wary distance, always.
One chestnut brown, one boot black,
calling to each other.

Looking Out over the Salt Marsh

My friend, who wanted to give her daughter
a sibling, five years ago, stopped by a partner's
hard no, discovered today that she's pregnant.
In her message, a hard edge of determination
has already left her voice, and I understand it.
So can anyone whose life has changed suddenly,
invisibly.
                    Fecundity, you ten-sided dice.
I fear menopause—the closing door—but also
every roll before that, every one of your faces.
I couldn't handle another child. What if I wanted
another child. Walking to the marsh, I felt bubbles
popping at my lips as another tampon drowned
with its mouth full of blood. Unexpected cramps,
warm wet. In the visitor center's bathroom, hand
splashed with bright blood viscous as unset jam
and hot, I saw another die face glittering red,
drying black.

Social media oracles tweet pronouncements
on my reasons for children, or none. Anyone's
children, or none. *Egoism. Overpopulation.*
Entrapment. Fulfillment. But did they decide
why their mothers? They didn't. (They couldn't
know, and will never know. That is the locket
of flesh, that is buried with the body.) Their mouths
gape and shut like the slow fish at the aquarium
as they speak of themselves and think of me.
Then they speak of me, thinking of themselves.
I hated infertility until I loved it. Last year, I
conceived twice and bled out twice, then realized
I was already happy.

Every Year, Another Invitation to Change Your Life

It's November. Sweetshrubs and spicebushes yellow,
   dropping bright pendulous leaves
       slowly as dipperfuls of honey.

     My elderly neighbor finds autumn depressing, saying
   everything dies in autumn,

       that the trees are catching fire
and burning to bones.
     I never understood this.

As a child I saw leaves fall like snowglobe storms
   or confetti drops on TV.

     I saw the old women of the forest shimmying like flappers
or rocking like congregants catching the Spirit,
       hands high above their heads.

Now I see them joyously cutting each other's hair,
   shaking off too-tight bras,

     baring private trunks striped with stretch marks
       for the sun to warm,
I see hackberry leaves taking each other's hands to jump together.

Autumn asks if I know
         how to cut my own hair. I used to. I don't.

God never rested on the seventh day, not here in the valley.
   It was the fourth day. She took off her bright clothes and fell
into bed.

Flower Moon

One way to light myself after darkness
is to fill my house with flowers—
branches of redbud and forsythia, violets and sugar
maple inflorescence stuffed
under locked door.

But I hesitate to look
at the green tongue of the violet.

Maybe it will lick my lips,
open my mouth with a dizzying frictive
pull, tease me,
make the sky teem again
with living joys.

From the highway where I've stopped the car,
I see a developed ridgetop.

It stands exposed and witless in the shadow
of the Smoky Mountains, its few trees
a white flag.
            The road itself occupies a developed ridge,
and from the mountains it too must appear sightless,
shorn.

        Nevertheless. Here
is my tired and beautiful skin,
my body full of knowledge,
on a ridge overlooking the spine of an ancient range.
Yonder are my mountains—unshorn, wise, free.

I am weightless, pale and freckled above the pines
          as buds burst and leaflets
sharpen and cleave.

Maple buds red as nipples. Poplars raising the green
mist of spring on the hillsides.

I who became a mother and left this world hold its invitation
in my body.

Let me remember myself
when I come into my daughter's kingdom.

The chickadees high up
in the pines,
how the gold star slowly rolled down,
burning my bare skin,

how I listened to the earth's silent
music,

and then stepped into the car,
shifted into third, and descended.

Few bother with the silence of the gods.
The silence that is the gestation
between two cataclysms.

While the sun sets among the mountains,
evening cool raises gooseflesh and bare nipples
beneath my linen shirt,
and makes me want to climb these pines
like a ladder.

Too old, now, to chase sunset,
I welcome the night wind.
Yes I say to the sun
who is going.

Acknowledgments

So many thanks to the following publications where these poems
first appeared:

"Children Are Not the Glue," *The Tusculum Review*
"Dawn with Holy Basil" and "Another Thing They Don't Tell
You," *The Pigeon Parade Quarterly*
"Driving the Baby," *Literary Mama*
"Exile," *MER: VOX Quarterly*
"First Sugar Moon of the Pandemic," *The Thinking Republic*
"First Unbroken Sleep," *Mutha Magazine*
"Flower Moon," *Broad River Review*
"In the Garden, Watching the Storm Come In," *Humana Obscura*
"Looking Out over the Salt Marsh," *ROOM Magazine*
"Ménière's Disease," *The Racket Journal* (nominated for a Pushcart
Prize)
"Pivoting in Appalachia," *Jet Fuel Review*
"Playing the Washboard" and "Sprouting Wand," *Canary*
"Thinking Big" and "New Myth," *Juke Joint*
"Trying," *Stirring: A Literary Collection*
"Vegetable X," *The Hopper* (nominated for a Pushcart Prize)
"The Work of Mothers," *Vita Brevis*
"Yard-Sitting during the Pandemic" and "Every Year, Another
Invitation to Change Your Life," *The Trumpeter*

"Tennessee Red Cob," a George Scarbrough Poetry Prize second-
place winner, was first published by *Appalachia Bare*.
"The Children of Asylum Seekers" is the 2019 winner of the
Knoxville Writer's Guild Poetry Contest.
"The Edinburgh Postnatal Depression Scale" is the 2022 winner
of *Beloit Poetry Journal*'s Adrienne Rich Poetry Award.

ANNA LAURA REEVE is a poet born and raised in East Tennessee. Winner of the 2022 Adrienne Rich Award, her work has been nominated twice for the Pushcart Prize and has appeared in *Beloit Poetry Journal, Terrain.org, Room, Still,* and others. She has an MA in literature and creative writing from the University of Tennessee, Knoxville.

Reaching the Shore of the Sea of Fertility
was designed, edited, and typeset by
Belle Point Press in Fort Smith, Arkansas, and was
printed and bound by Bookmobile in Minneapolis, Minnesota.

The text is set in Arno Pro.
Cover titles are set in Joanna Sans Nova and Mr Eaves Sans.

The mission of Belle Point Press is to celebrate the
literary culture and community
of the American Mid-South:
all its paradoxes and contradictions,
all the ways it gets us home.
Visit us at
www.bellepointpress.com.

Fort Smith, Arkansas